CW01663149

Cold Han Heart

Nala Shaw

BookLeaf Publishing

Cold Hands, Warm Heart © 2022 Nala Shaw

All rights reserved.

No part of this publication may be reproduced, stored in a retrieval system, or transmitted, in any form or by any means, electronic, mechanical, photocopying, recording or otherwise, without the prior written permission of the presenters.

Nala Shaw asserts the moral right to be identified as author of this work.

Presentation by *BookLeaf Publishing*

Web: www.bookleafpub.com

E-mail: info@bookleafpub.com

ISBN: 9789357695329

First edition 2022

To my husband, my sister and my beautiful cats.

Masks

I wore one to blend in
To capture the external validation
I desperately seek

I swapped it at home for one who spoke no
English
Who did as it was expected
Obliging and dutiful

Bare faced, I am unhappy
With my too many masks

I take sertraline to stop this obsession
Who am I?
Who should I be?

At night my mask conjures the wildest of
dreams
In which I am the happiest

The mould is setting into my final form.

Booty Call

I could really do with those kisses.
And with a good, hard, scratching, biting, dirty, rough, passionate, s***ty, filthy, exhausting, fulfilling f**k.

Game on.

New Crush

You used the word apropos and I fell in love
with you
Your response: I appreciate that you appreciated
it
You knew you had me then

Actions and Reactions

If you treat people like animals
They will behave so
Bite you or whimper as submissive

Treat them how you want them to be

Be nice if you want them to be nice?
No, that's conditional

Take what you want from them?
Bullying.

Then how?

Nurture your own happiness and you will treat others right
The reaction begins within you.

A Good Year

The wine I brought to drink with you
I downed the bottle alone
Sweet taste and my bitter thoughts
Fully bodied, numbing my loneliness

Crazy Cat Lady

My antidepressants since May 2020
Floofy, four legged rulers of the world

Demand love, only when you want it
Anything you want, you got it

Make me feel insignificant, I need to be humbled
Yes, I am here to serve you
Crazy cat lady.

Happy Anniversary

Annual sex
Greying knickers with frilling hems

Holes in your boxers
Baby gorilla legs

Dad body but we got no kids
We'll do better next year

I love you

Don't be Anxious

Just don’t be anxious, you said
And my anxiety laughed

Choose to be happy
I am trying, believe me

What can I do? I feel so helpless,
I’ll get you a kitten.

Sisters

To those who left their violent husbands
To those leaving arranged marriages
To those single mums
And working mums
You are brave and strong with the best days
ahead of you

Self Control

I delete your number to stop texting you
But end up emailing you
I delete my apps
But download them back for you

You are the dopamine I crave
I'm not even sure why you're so special
You caught my feelings at their most venerable
Now you have a hold on me

My obsession, until my tears dry out
And then obsess some more

My heavy heart adds to the ice cream weight
I buy no snacks to prevent over eating
But I end up high, taking a spoon to the peanut butter jar
8 portions in a packet? More like 30 minutes to finish off

Heart breaker, smile stealer
Depressed and pining for you

Baby

I didn't ovulate
And your sperm count was 4
The app says I'm fertile
Quick! Let us f**k

Perform for me homosapien
Impregnate me with your swimmers
Send two to the right and two to the left
Ambush that zygote

Give me a baby, please

The Job

New rotation
Spent three months bowing to another Queen
Now, new names to learn, all 14 of them

He calls your name wrong
I answer to anything I laugh, *nervous*
Your name is like N followed by a series of letters
He says jokingly. Innocent.
I laugh along hesitantly
It can only get better

Endometriosis

Womans' pain
Dismissed
Mefenamic acid
Time of the month

Tears, discomfort
Stoicism, defeat

Sought help, covid.
Two years wait
Surgery, extensive disease.

33, sub fertile
Losing my youth
Geriatric mother,
When I get there.

Sister

Five years my senior
Wiser than her years
Tret me like her baby doll
Alleviated all my fears

Took a beating so I was protected
Carried me home with a broken foot
Endured an arranged marriage for 22 years
Supported me to marry who I wanted

You needed to be strong and hard
While my heart remained on my sleeve
You deserve the best sister award
I'm going to give you a good life, you'll see

New Money

Holidays during covid
San pelligrino sparkling water
What is this high tea you talk about?

Your first car was what?
Skiing trip this easter?
South of France this summer?
Daddy knows who?

Keep your head down, they will smell you are
poor.

Dichotomy

One type A, go getter, selfish, lustrous,
dopamine chasing CEO
The other authentic, loving, parasympathetic,
wise friend

The ADHD, Ritalin crunching, self-preserving
leader
Versus the calm, thought out observer, from the
side line

The prize enjoyer, the competition winner, the
intimidator
And the one who appreciates the journey, the
healer of pain

The dichotomy between ego and soul

Soulless

To be weary of differences is natural
Racism is expected, normal
We crave belonging
Accept me into your tribe

Forget race, or gender, but social class
Don’t blackball me now
I have money don’t you know

Let me into your boys’ club
And I will become like you
Pull the ladder up and look down on a former
version of me

Woke

Anti-Karen
Reddit scroller
Labor voting
Boomer hatin'
Lefty liberal

Oat milk drinking
Vegan eating
Recycling queen

Bicycle riding
Air travel avoiding
Advocate for mother Earth

Immigrant sympathiser
War opposer
Weed smoking hippie

Jacinda supporter
Trudeau fan
No to Donald Trump

Take the knee
Let him breath
Don't shoot, please

Snooze

Park your nose in my ear canal to keep it warm
Hold me close for two more minutes while we
lay in bed
Alexa, snooze alarm.

Morning stretches in bed
Curl those toes
Let me hold you like a jet pack
Avoid my morning breath

Cats on the bed
Purring for morning treats
Wrapped around your arm
Now here, you must remain
Alexa, snooze alarm five more minutes.

Women

Divya, the kindest soul
Halima, the best sister
Hannah, my mushroom expert
Hira, you taught and looked after me a lot
Isa, for being an aspiration
Jayoti, with your infectious laughter
Kimberley, my childhood sweetheart
Mariam, so much wiser than your years
Musfirah, the cutest nerd
My mum and mum in law. Thank you
Rachael, one of the strongest of people

Love for you all.

Haiku4u

I have concluded
That animals are better
Than selfish humans

Milton Keynes UK
Ingram Content Group UK Ltd.
UKHW050224250624
444652UK00015B/749

9 789357 695329